*Accep* ... *, y*

# Acceptance Therapy

written by
**Lisa O. Engelhardt**

illustrated by
**R.W. Alley**

ONE
CARING
PLACE

Abbey Press

Text © 1992 Lisa O. Engelhardt
Illustrations © 1992 St. Meinrad Archabbey
Published by One Caring Place
Abbey Press
St. Meinrad, Indiana 47577

Library of Congress Catalog Number
92-71076


ISBN 0-87029-245-5


Printed in the United States of America

# Foreword

We want to be in control. We want our life to follow the mental master plan we've devised that ultimately leads to Real Happiness. But circumstances—loss, illness, unresolvable problems, burnout, addiction, monotony—often foil our plan. And we struggle to reconcile ourselves to the limitations and the brokenness of our life.

*Acceptance Therapy* is for those who have trouble letting go—who find themselves clinging to their own life-blueprint instead of cooperating with the fluidity of grace. Taking inspiration from Vincent P. Collins's best-selling booklet *Acceptance*, this collection of guidelines encourages you to plunge into the reality of your life right now—by accepting yourself, accepting others' personal choices, accepting mystery, and, above all, accepting the Love that is the current of all life.

Practicing a daily habit of acceptance may not change the circumstances of your life, but it can gradually transform the way you experience life. For anyone who wants to be more in tune with the harmony of life, this book will strike a resonating chord.

## 1.

Acceptance doesn't mean giving in or giving up; it means giving all—your hopes, sorrows, worries—to God.

**2.**

Stop living in a past that is gone and a tomorrow that is yet to come. Life is only this place, this time, this breath—right now.

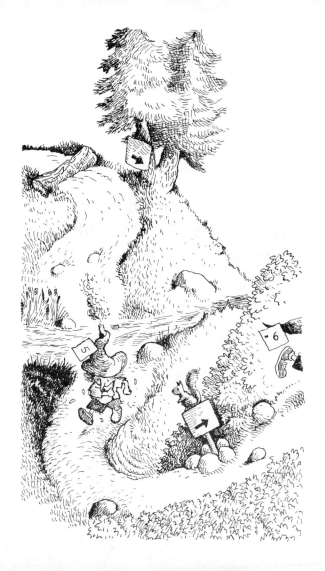

## 3.

An attitude of acceptance is a constant prayer. Turn your life over to God with every beat of your heart.

*4.*

Acceptance is the only real source of serenity. You can live with your brokenness and in spite of it.

## 5.

You may not be able to do anything about a problem today. When that happens, accept it and forget it.

## 6.

When you have done the best you can, let go. Leave the rest to the One whose love and wisdom envelop everything you do.

## 7.

Accept yourself. Your Maker took delight in the mere idea of you before you even existed.

## 8.

You are constantly becoming.
Honor all that you have been, all
that you are, all that you will be.

## 9.

*Stop trying to be perfect. You have everything you need to be who you are supposed to be.*

The Hat shop

## 10.

Accept your humanity;
you're allowed to stumble.

## 11.

Accept your divinity; the God within you empowers you to pick yourself up again.

## 12.

Ignore unfair criticism.
Others can't hurt you unless
you let them.

## 13.

Don't try to please everybody.
Charity begins at home—
please yourself.

## 14.

Don't force your good intentions on others. You can't help them unless they want you to.

## 15.

Befriend your anger. Listen—
it has much to teach you.

## 16.

Set the compass of your soul toward forgiveness. It will help you to find your way out of bitterness.

## 17.

Give others freedom. When you hold them captive to your own wishes, you destroy them.

## 18.

Trust in God. God's love prevails throughout every moment of your existence.

## 19.

When evil seems to be winning over good, remember that creation is not yet finished. You can help to shape creation for good.

## 20.

Don't disown any part of yourself. What you may consider "garbage" can be the ground of new life.

## 21.

Trust in the future. Recall the times you've seen good emerge from tragedy, new life rise out of dying.

## 22.

When darkness surrounds
you and extinguishes all hope,
trust that God will rekindle
your spirit.

## 23.

Accept your path, with its many twists and turns. The adventure is in the journey, not the arriving.

CLICK

## 24.

You cannot change circumstances
or other people. If you don't like
the way your life looks, try
changing the way you look
at life.

## 25.

Step away from your life to look at it. Life is like a painting— messy close up, but blending into a harmonious whole from a distance.

## 26.

Accept suffering. It can stretch
your heart to make room for
greater love and joy.

## 27.

Be open to growth. The hard
seeds of misfortune blossom into
the flowers of courage and
compassion.

# 28.

Contentment doesn't mean
getting all you want, but
enjoying what you have.
Don't postpone enjoyment!

## 29.

If you feel yourself unraveling,
get rest and play. You need
re-creation each day.

## 30.

Retreat from the world's noise
and the clamor of your own
worries. In silence you can hear
the whisper of the Infinite.

## 31.

Relax and breathe. Breathe
in the love instilled into this
speck of time and creation.
Breathe out fear.

## 32.

Immerse yourself in nature. When you can't be outdoors, feel deep within you the cleansing breeze, the lake's calm, the bud's promise.

## 33.

Place yourself in the arms of God.
God will cradle you and sing you
a lullaby of love.

## 34.

Grasp for happiness and it will elude you. Be still and at one with life, and happiness will alight upon you.

## 35.

Give thanks for everything;
a grateful heart yields a harvest
of acceptance.

**Lisa O. Engelhardt** is editorial director for Product Development at Abbey Press. She is the author of *Finding the Serenity of Acceptance* and *Happy Birthday Therapy* and a co-author of *Anger Therapy*. She lives with her husband and three children in Lawrenceburg, Indiana.

Illustrator for the Abbey Press Elf-help Books, **R.W. Alley** also illustrates and writes children's books. He lives in Barrington, Rhode Island, with his wife, daughter, and son.

# The Story of the Abbey Press Elves

The engaging figures that populate the Abbey Press "elf-help" line of publications and products first appeared in 1987 on the pages of a small self-help book called *Be-good-to-yourself Therapy*. Shaped by the publishing staff's vision and defined in R.W. Alley's inventive illustrations, they lived out author Cherry Hartman's gentle, self-nurturing advice with charm, poignancy, and humor.

Reader response was so enthusiastic that more Elf-help Books were soon under way, a still-growing series that has inspired a line of related gift products.

The especially endearing character featured in the early books—sporting a cap with a mood-changing candle in its peak—has since been joined by a spirited female elf with flowers in her hair.

These two exuberant, sensitive, resourceful, kindhearted, lovable sprites, along with their lively elfin community, reveal what's truly important as they offer messages of joy and wonder, playfulness and co-creation, wholeness and serenity, the miracle of life and the mystery of God's love.

With wisdom and whimsy, these little creatures with long noses demonstrate the elf-help way to a rich and fulfilling life.

# *Elf-help Books*

**...adding "a little character" and a lot of help to self-help reading!**

**Be-good-to-your-family Therapy**
#20154    $4.95    ISBN 0-87029-300-1

**Stress Therapy**
#20153    $4.95    ISBN 0-87029-301-X

**Making-sense-out-of-suffering Therapy**
#20156    $4.95    ISBN 0-87029-296-X

**Get Well Therapy**
#20157    $4.95    ISBN 0-87029-297-8

**Anger Therapy**
#20127    $4.95    ISBN 0-87029-292-7

**Caregiver Therapy**
#20164    $4.95    ISBN 0-87029-285-4

**Self-esteem Therapy**
#20165    $4.95    ISBN 0-87029-280-3

**Take-charge-of-your-life Therapy**
#20168    $4.95    ISBN 0-87029-271-4

**Work Therapy**
#20166    $4.95    ISBN 0-87029-276-5

**Everyday-courage Therapy**
#20167    $4.95    ISBN 0-87029-274-9

**Peace Therapy**
#20176     $4.95     ISBN 0-87029-273-0

**Friendship Therapy**
#20174     $4.95     ISBN 0-87029-270-6

**Christmas Therapy** (color edition)
#20175     $5.95     ISBN 0-87029-268-4

**Grief Therapy**
#20178     $4.95     ISBN 0-87029-267-6

**More Be-good-to-yourself Therapy**
#20180     $3.95     ISBN 0-87029-262-5

**Happy Birthday Therapy**
#20181     $4.95     ISBN 0-87029-260-9

**Forgiveness Therapy**
#20184     $4.95     ISBN 0-87029-258-7

**Keep-life-simple Therapy**
#20185     $4.95     ISBN 0-87029-257-9

**Be-good-to-your-body Therapy**
#20188     $4.95     ISBN 0-87029-255-2

**Celebrate-your-womanhood Therapy**
#20189     $4.95     ISBN 0-87029-254-4

**Acceptance Therapy** (color edition)
#20182     $5.95     ISBN 0-87029-259-5

**Acceptance Therapy**
#20190     $4.95     ISBN 0-87029-245-5

**Keeping-up-your-spirits Therapy**
#20195     $4.95     ISBN 0-87029-242-0

**Play Therapy**
#20200     $4.95     ISBN 0-87029-233-1

**Slow-down Therapy**
#20203     $4.95     ISBN 0-87029-229-3

**One-day-at-a-time Therapy**
#20204     $4.95     ISBN 0-87029-228-5

**Prayer Therapy**
#20206     $4.95     ISBN 0-87029-225-0

**Be-good-to-your-marriage Therapy**
#20205     $4.95     ISBN 0-87029-224-2

**Be-good-to-yourself Therapy** (hardcover)
#20196     $10.95    ISBN 0-87029-243-9

**Be-good-to-yourself Therapy**
#20255     $4.95     ISBN 0-87029-209-9

Available at your favorite bookstore or directly from us at: One Caring Place, Abbey Press Publications, St. Meinrad, IN 47577. Or call 1-800-325-2511.